ANIMAL SIDEKICKS

NEON SQUID

Contents

4   What is Symbiosis?

6   The Tarantula and the Frog
8   The Coyote and the Badger
10 The Bats and the Figs
12 The Hippo and the Terrapins
14 The Vampire Finch and the Booby
16 The Tiger Orchid and the Tree
18 The Ants and the Aphids
20 The Zebras and the Ostriches
22 The Chimpanzee and the Fruit Tree
24 The Cow and the Egrets
26 The Oxpeckers and the Rhinos
28 The Carrion Beetle and the Mites
30 The Skink and the Tree
32 The Clownfish and the Anemone
34 The Skua and the Puffin
36 The Snail and the Hermit Crab
38 The Bees and the Flowers
40 The Honeyguide and the Humans

42 The Spider Crab and the Algae
44 The Capybara and the Cattle Tyrant
46 The Humpback Whale and the Barnacles
48 The Ants and the Fungus
50 The Crayfish and the Worms
52 The Elephant Shrew and the Lily
54 The Giant Tube Worm and the Bacteria
56 The Human and the Head Lice
58 The Grouper and the Octopus
60 The Woolly Bat and the Pitcher Plant
62 The Carrier Crab and the Urchin
64 The Zebra and the Wildebeest
66 The Cuckoo and the Reed Warbler
68 The Hummingbirds and the Flowers
70 The Eel and the Wrasse
72 The Warthog and the Mongooses

74 The Leafflower Moth and the Tree

76 The Vampire Bats and the Pigs

78 The Mosquito and the Orchid

80 The Manta Ray and the Remoras

82 The Birds and the Trees

84 The Large Blue and the Red Ant

86 The Pack Rat and the Pseudoscorpion

88 The Wolves and the Hyena

90 The Crab Spiders and the Flowers

92 The Human and the Dogs

94 The Ants and the Acacia

96 The Woodpeckers and the Cactus

98 The Human and the Corn

100 The Squirrel and the Oak Tree

102 The Tortoise and the Beetle

104 The Sloth and the Algae

106 The Green Chromide and the Orange Chromide

108 The Lemur and the Palm

110 The Lemon Ants and the Devil's Garden

112 The Cowbird and the Yellowthroat

114 The Boxer Crab and the Anemones

116 The Swift Parrot and the Blue Gum

118 The Pilot Fish and the Great White

120 The Drongo and the Meerkats

122 The Goby and the Shrimp

124 Glossary

126 Index

128 Acknowledgments

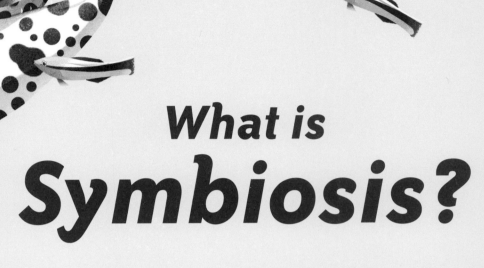

What is Symbiosis?

Unless they're trying to eat one another, most animals want nothing to do with each other. Creatures of all kinds tend to stick to their own. Monkeys hang out with monkeys, salmon with salmon, peacocks with peacocks, and so on. This book is about more unusual cases. It looks at examples of **symbiosis**, which is where different species of animals, plants, and other living organisms form interesting relationships.

When most people think of symbiosis, they think only of win-win situations. There are plenty of those waiting for you in this book, from mongooses cleaning warthogs to frogs guarding spider eggs. But symbiosis includes much more than happy pals: It can be any long interaction between

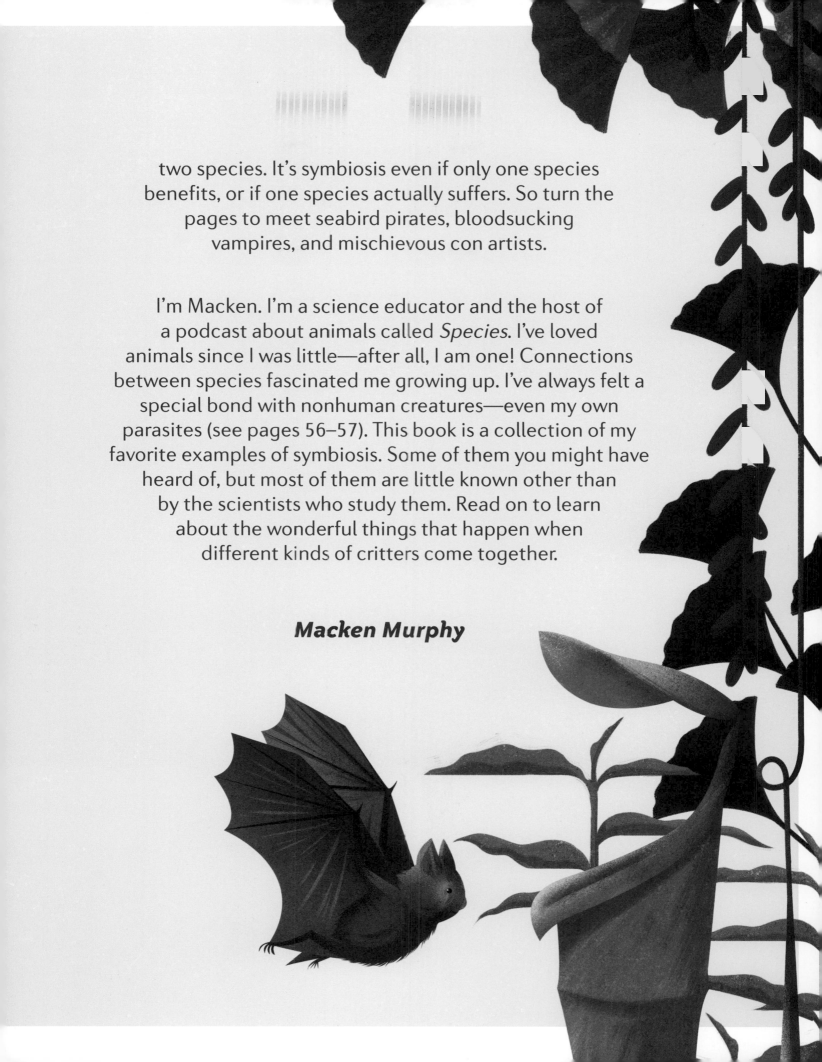

two species. It's symbiosis even if only one species benefits, or if one species actually suffers. So turn the pages to meet seabird pirates, bloodsucking vampires, and mischievous con artists.

I'm Macken. I'm a science educator and the host of a podcast about animals called *Species*. I've loved animals since I was little—after all, I am one! Connections between species fascinated me growing up. I've always felt a special bond with nonhuman creatures—even my own parasites (see pages 56–57). This book is a collection of my favorite examples of symbiosis. Some of them you might have heard of, but most of them are little known other than by the scientists who study them. Read on to learn about the wonderful things that happen when different kinds of critters come together.

Macken Murphy

The Tarantula and the Frog

Unusual eggs, right? They look odd because tarantulas keep them in a silken egg sac.

Babysitter

While the tarantula guards the door, the frog keeps an eye on the eggs. Ants sneak by, intending to eat the tarantula's offspring, but the frog eats the ants before they get a chance.

Oops

These two aren't home 24/7, and sometimes they bump into each other when out running errands. Unfortunately, this tarantula hunts other frogs and can mistake its friend for food!

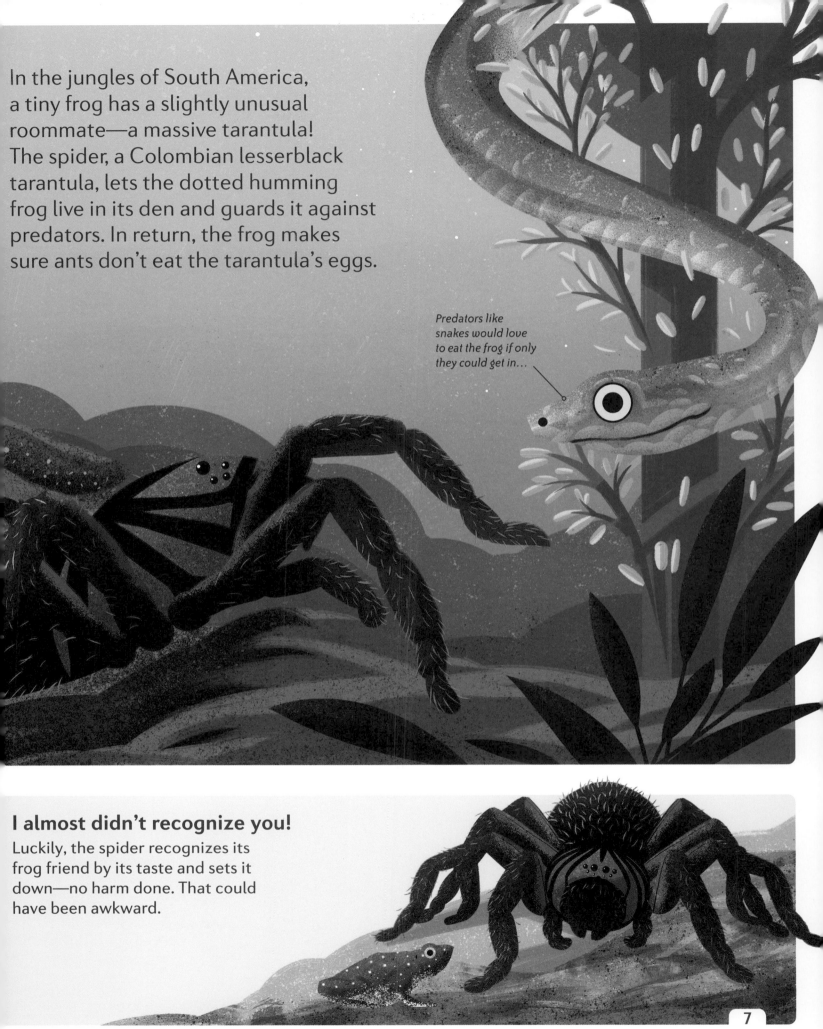

In the jungles of South America, a tiny frog has a slightly unusual roommate—a massive tarantula! The spider, a Colombian lesserblack tarantula, lets the dotted humming frog live in its den and guards it against predators. In return, the frog makes sure ants don't eat the tarantula's eggs.

Predators like snakes would love to eat the frog if only they could get in...

I almost didn't recognize you!

Luckily, the spider recognizes its frog friend by its taste and sets it down—no harm done. That could have been awkward.

The Coyote

Coyote

and the Badger

Badger

Sensing danger, the prairie dog bolts toward the surface (bad idea).

Prairie dogs raise their young underground in special chambers.

Playmates

This form of teamwork was thought to be purely business, but in 2020 a video of a coyote and a badger playing together went viral.

Better together

Studies have shown that coyotes that team up with badgers catch more ground squirrels than coyotes that hunt alone. On average the coyote-badger dream team catches a third more!

On the prairies of North America, coyotes and badgers often team up to form impressive hunting duos. While the coyote patrols aboveground, the badger scurries after prairie dogs underground. Whoever catches something first gets the spoils.

Prairie dogs have different chambers for eating, sleeping, and even going to the bathroom!

On the menu

Coyotes and badgers aren't especially picky, but their dinner of choice is usually made up of prairie dogs or ground squirrels—two den-dwelling species of the plains.

Prairie dog

Ground squirrel

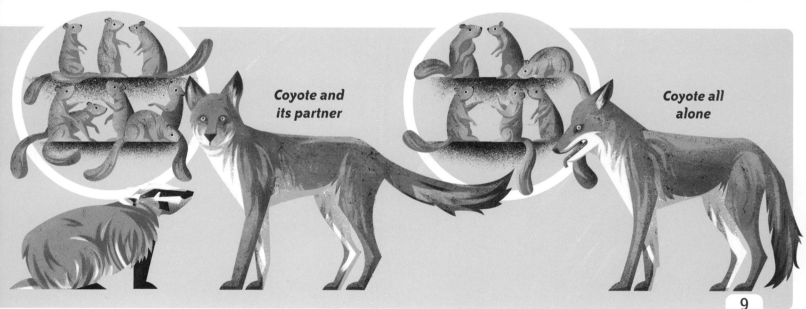

Coyote and its partner

Coyote all alone

9

The Bats and the Figs

Lots of things in the natural world try to avoid being eaten, but these figs are hoping to become bat food! When bats eat figs, they unintentionally act as fig farmers, planting seeds across the forest.

Yellow-eared bat

Designed to be delicious

Because fig trees benefit from bats eating their fruit, the figs have changed over time, or **evolved**, to make sure they're super tasty.

Bat airlines

When the bat eats a fig, it carries its seeds in its poop. The bat gets a meal. The fig seeds get a ride!

Echo detectors

In the dark of night, bats can't see with their eyes very well, so they use a special system called echolocation. They make high-pitched squeaks that bounce back to them off of different objects. This way, they know what's there.

Different figs, different species

Some fig tree species are so reliant on bats for reproduction that they've evolved to attract *specific* bat species. Notice how different types of bat are eating different types of fig?

Great fruit-eating bat

Leaf-nosed bat

Planting with poop

When bats poop, the seed goes through them unharmed. They've brought the seed to a new location, and their poop helps **fertilize** it—meaning it creates perfect growing conditions.

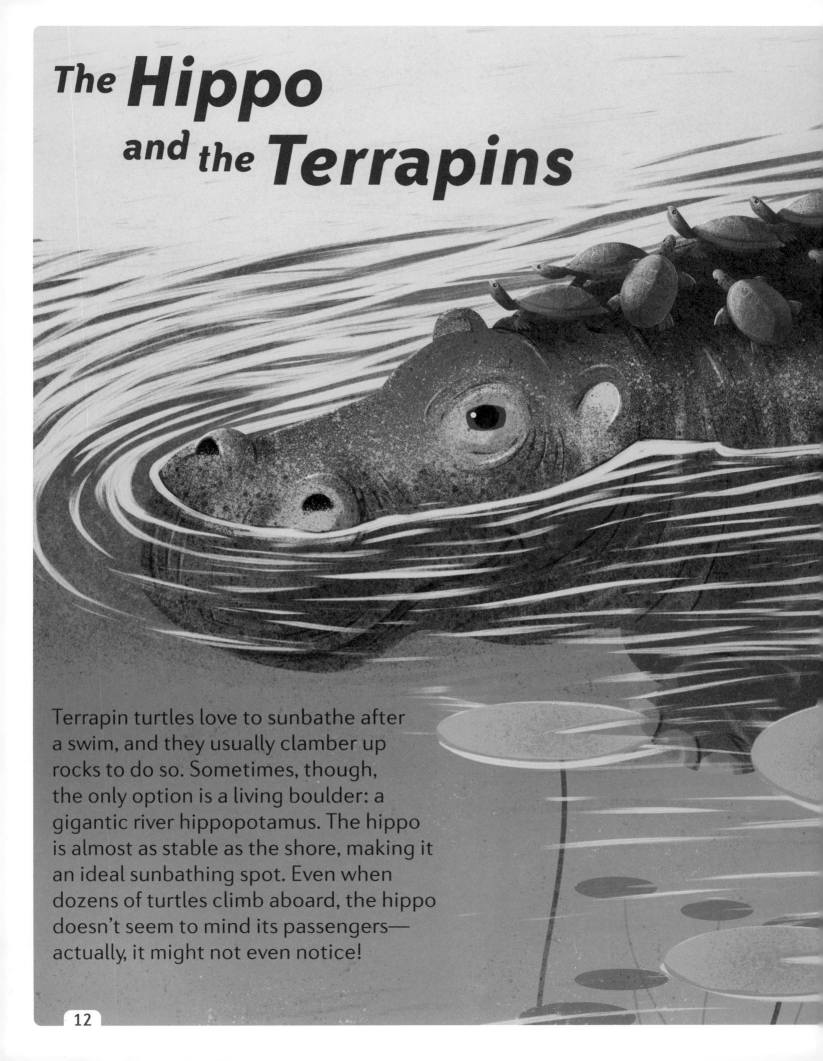

The Hippo
and the Terrapins

Terrapin turtles love to sunbathe after a swim, and they usually clamber up rocks to do so. Sometimes, though, the only option is a living boulder: a gigantic river hippopotamus. The hippo is almost as stable as the shore, making it an ideal sunbathing spot. Even when dozens of turtles climb aboard, the hippo doesn't seem to mind its passengers—actually, it might not even notice!

Even on a hot day in Africa, the waters can get a little too chilly for a terrapin.

Heating up

Terrapins, like all reptiles, have to use heat from their environment to keep their bodies at a good temperature. To stay warm, they regularly leave the water and bask in the sun. It's like they're charging their batteries for their next activity.

The Vampire Finch and the Booby

A tropical paradise is the last place you would expect to find vampires, but on the Galápagos Islands bloodthirsty birds feed in broad daylight. These finches drink blood from large seabirds known as boobies, who—strangely—don't seem to mind it.

Trusting friends

Researchers suspect these finches used to eat parasites off the boobies' bodies. Over time, the boobies learned to trust the finches and happily let the little birds land on their backs and pick through their feathers. Eventually, the finches started backstabbing their trusting allies—literally!

The Nazca booby is one of several species that are victims of the vampire finches.

The vampire finch's sharp beak doubles as a scalpel.

The **Tiger Orchid** and the **Tree**

We tend to think of orchids as flowers you might give to your mom for Mother's Day, but if you want to give someone a tiger orchid, you'd better have a delivery truck ready. This plant is the largest orchid on Earth! Though it can live under a variety of conditions, it prefers to grow in trees as an **epiphyte**: a plant that grows on other plants. Thanks to the tree, the orchid gets a great spot high up in the forest where it can get lots of light. It doesn't even need to reach the ground—it has special roots that absorb rainfall from the surface of the tree's bark.

This *flower* is also known as the "**queen** of the **orchids**."

Taller than a giraffe

The tallest giraffe ever measured was almost 20 ft (6 m) tall, but tiger orchids can be 25 ft (7.5 m) high!

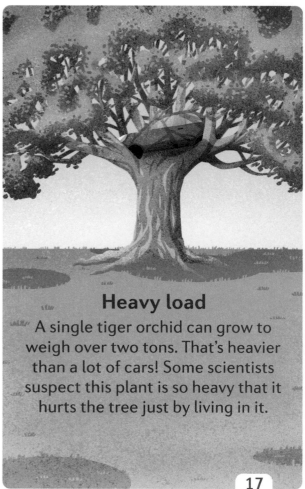

Heavy load

A single tiger orchid can grow to weigh over two tons. That's heavier than a lot of cars! Some scientists suspect this plant is so heavy that it hurts the tree just by living in it.

The Ants and the Aphids

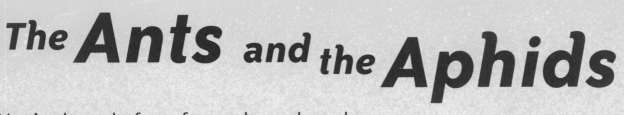

You've heard of ant farms, but what about ant farmers? The yellow meadow ant is to the root aphid what the human is to the dairy cow. These ants manage enormous underground herds of root aphids. When they're hungry, the ants "milk" the aphids, drinking honeydew from their rear ends. The ants get a reliable food supply, while the aphids get security (and free air travel—but more on that in a moment).

Out to pasture

Dairy cows and root aphids both feed on grass—just different parts. These aphids eat grass roots underground. It's not a coincidence that the ant colony has roots crossing through all of its tunnels: The ants designed their home to be the ideal aphid habitat.

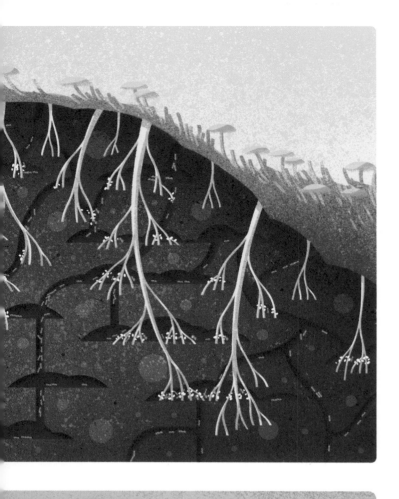

Meet the team

Below, we have an aphid, an ant worker, and an ant queen. The queen is the mother of all the workers, who work together because they're related. In nature, if you share the same family genes, you're on the same team!

Aphid   *Ant worker*   *Ant queen*

Milking aphids

Root aphids secrete a sugary liquid called honeydew. Yellow meadow ants just have to "milk" them for a tasty drink!

Flying ants

A young queen ant can fly to a new location when it's time to begin a new ant colony. When she leaves, she will bring aphid eggs with her so she can start her own farm.

The Zebras and the Ostriches

Ostriches are among the best lookouts on Earth. Their towering height gives them a wonderful vantage point, and their lemon-sized eyes give them excellent vision. Zebras are often seen in the company of ostriches. Some scientists have wondered if ostriches use their superior sight to give zebras a heads-up when a predator appears on the horizon.

Zebras might return the favor with their stronger hearing and sense of smell.

These chicks hatched from massive eggs—one ostrich egg is the size of 22 chicken eggs!

Predator spotted

An ostrich can see a predator—such as a lion or hyena—long before any zebra could hope to. Its startled reaction tips off everybody in the area. Thanks to the ostrich, everybody has time to get themselves to safety.

Among land animals, ostriches have the largest eyes in the world.

The Chimpanzee and the Fruit Tree

Chimpanzees swing through the trees of tropical Africa, foraging for fruits. The trees give the chimpanzees a place to sleep, safe traveling routes, and nourishing food. The chimps, in return, give the trees new life: When they eat the trees' fruit, they also eat the seeds, and when they poop, they plant new trees!

Chimps nest in trees.

Fruitful harvest

Contrary to popular belief, chimpanzees don't just eat bananas. Wild chimpanzees eat a wide variety of fruits you might not be able to find at your local supermarket.

Fig

Musanga cecropioides

22

Figs make up half of a chimp's diet.

Chimps eat 80 different types of fruit.

Traveling through the chimpanzee's gut makes seeds more likely to develop, and the dung acts as a fertilizer upon exit!

Drypetes afzelii

Custard apple

Oil palm

As cows trample through fields, they startle bugs that live in the grass, flushing them from their hiding places. When the little creatures take flight, they get a nasty shock. Egrets, a type of small heron, are right there waiting for them! They pluck the bugs from the skies as soon as they get the chance. The cow serves its egret followers a free meal with every step, but it's unclear if the cow gets any benefit from this arrangement.

The Cow and the Egrets

A moo-ving partnership

Researchers estimate that an egret is almost four times more effective at hunting bugs with the help of a cow. This means that for every ten bugs a solo egret catches, an egret with a cow will get nearly 40!

Dinner with cow helper

Eating alone

The Oxpeckers and the Rhinos

Oxpeckers ride rhinos across sub-Saharan Africa, eating ticks off the backs of their big buddies. But these birds aren't actually effective as a means of pest control for the rhinos. Instead, they're lookouts!

Flying alarms

Rhinos can't see well, but oxpeckers have excellent vision. This allows them to act as sentries, quietly hissing if predators come near.

Selfish helpers

Oxpeckers wait until the ticks have filled up with blood to make their meal as juicy as possible. That's like waiting to stop a bank robber until after they've emptied the vault, then taking the money for yourself!

An oxpecker can eat over 100 ticks a day!

Earwax extractors

As if the oxpecker's penchant for ticks wasn't already gross enough, this bird likes to eat them with a side of earwax! (Scientists have no clue whether this hurts or helps the rhinos.)

The oxpecker pays for its meal by acting as the rhino's security detail. The bird must keep a vigilant eye out for any predators who could attack a young rhino.

The oxpecker's Swahili name, "askari wa kifaru," fits perfectly. It means "rhino's guard."

The Carrion Beetle and the Mites

The carrion beetle is a bus to the buffet. It picks up hordes of mites and carries them to a dead animal. The mites climb down and eat any fly eggs on the corpse, while the carrion beetle eats the meat itself. Mites get a free ride to a free meal, and in return they get rid of any flies that might compete with the carrion beetle for the tasty meat.

1. Setting the table

Shortly after a mouse dies it will be visited by flies. They lay their eggs in the flesh of the dead rodent. (Because flies lay eggs in meat, some scientists hundreds of years ago thought corpses transformed into flies!)

3. Disembarking

Arriving by the mouse, the mites climb down from the beetles. They have an important job to do.

4. Killing the competition

The mites want to eat the young flies! They set upon the eggs and hatched larvae, who are too helpless to defend themselves.

2. All aboard!

After the flies leave, a pair of carrion beetles (who have sniffed out the corpse from miles away) arrive at the dead mouse with packs of hungry mites on board.

5. Magnificent meatball

The carrion beetles now have the mouse all to themselves. They take it underground and turn it into a meatball before laying their eggs on it. A perfect snack for their own babies.

Carrion beetle larvae

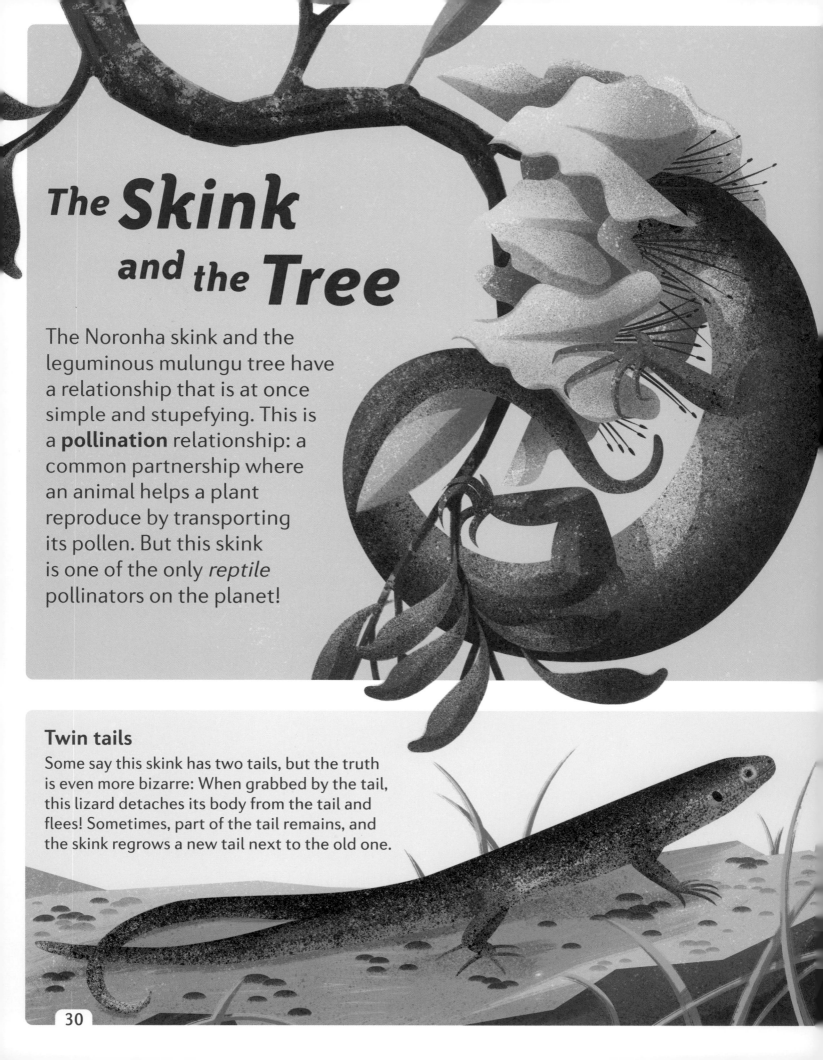

The Skink and the Tree

The Noronha skink and the leguminous mulungu tree have a relationship that is at once simple and stupefying. This is a **pollination** relationship: a common partnership where an animal helps a plant reproduce by transporting its pollen. But this skink is one of the only *reptile* pollinators on the planet!

Twin tails

Some say this skink has two tails, but the truth is even more bizarre: When grabbed by the tail, this lizard detaches its body from the tail and flees! Sometimes, part of the tail remains, and the skink regrows a new tail next to the old one.

Messy eater

The skink sticks its face into the flower to get its delicious nectar. When it does this, it gets covered in powdery pollen. This means when it visits the next flower, it will drop off some pollen, allowing the flower to create new seeds.

What's a lizard doing way up here?

This skink is only 3 in (7 cm) long, but it often has to climb nearly 40 ft (12 m) up a tree to get its food. That would be like you having to scale a bridge just to eat your breakfast!

The Clownfish and the Anemone

Clownfish leftovers are the perfect anemone snack. Fish scraps fall right into the anemone's clutches.

Some believe the clownfish might serve as a lure for the anemone's prey, such as other fish or crabs.

Venomous fortress

Each tentacle is loaded with tiny, venomous harpoons that shoot into trespassers. This keeps the clownfish safe from potential predators, who fear the anemone's dreaded sting!

At the bottom of shallow tropical seas, anemones offer clownfish a cozy home with a built-in security system. Meanwhile, the clownfish pay rent by helping the anemones breathe, protecting them from butterflyfish, and by feeding them (somewhat strange) meals.

Unusual armor

The clownfish need not fear the anemone's venom. Each clownfish has a layer of mucus that protects it from the anemone's harpoons. Over time, the anemone learns to not even bother stinging its colorful tenants.

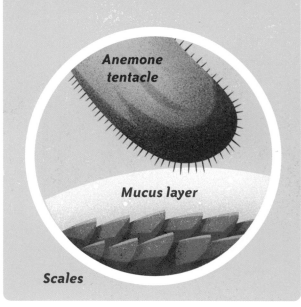

Anemone tentacle

Mucus layer

Scales

Clownfish poop is an excellent fertilizer. It helps anemones grow.

If a butterflyfish tries to eat the anemone, the clownfish will chase it off!

Partying all night long

As night falls, oxygen levels in the water reduce, and the anemone needs more water to breathe. Clownfish dance all night to stir up the water, ensuring their anemone gets enough oxygen.

The Skua and the Puffin

Above the frigid waters of the northern Atlantic Ocean, a career criminal scans the skies for potential marks. The skua, a type of seabird, is a **kleptoparasite**—an animal that survives by stealing from others. It's hungry for fresh fish, and it prefers to get it the easy way: Up to 95% of the skua's meals are taken straight from the mouths of other birds!

Today's victim
This puffin has just caught some lunch. But trouble is incoming. The puffin is one of many seabird species terrorized by the skua.

The lesser of two losses

The skua swoops down and grabs the fish from the puffin's beak. The puffin doesn't resist the thieving skua. Why risk it? It would have little hope of winning a fight—it evolved to catch fish, while the skua evolved for aerial battle and could kill and eat the puffin! It's an easy choice: miss a meal or gamble with your life.

The getaway

The skua flies off, heist complete. It will plot another as soon as it gets hungry again. All parasites are thieves in some sense, but few make this more apparent than the skua!

The Snail and the Hermit Crab

Some shells are just too big...

Sea snail (still alive)

No vacancy

Sometimes, one hermit crab will wait next to a slightly bigger one. The smaller crab hopes that the bigger crab will move out of its shell, allowing it to move in. Occasionally, multiple crabs line up in this manner, resulting in a crab conga line!

Every hermit crab's home is a hand-me-down. These crustaceans have a soft, vulnerable lower body, so they can't survive without a shell. They look for used sea snail shells to act as their mobile homes, and they're always trying to upgrade: As they grow bigger, they need bigger shells!

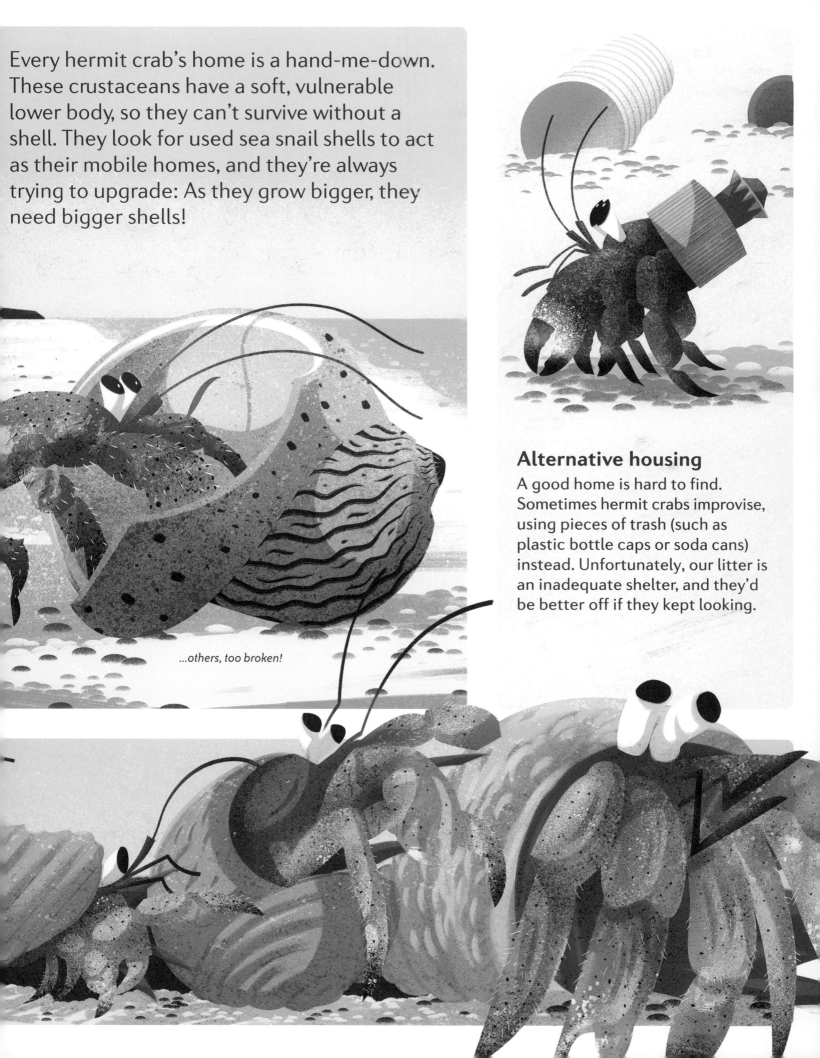

...others, too broken!

Alternative housing

A good home is hard to find. Sometimes hermit crabs improvise, using pieces of trash (such as plastic bottle caps or soda cans) instead. Unfortunately, our litter is an inadequate shelter, and they'd be better off if they kept looking.

The Bees and the Flowers

When you see a bee buzz on by, it's hard to imagine it's doing one of nature's most important jobs—but it is. Bees spend their days flitting from flower to flower, searching for tasty nectar. They **pollinate** the flowers as they go, helping plants make more plants. Without bees, you wouldn't have as much food on your plate: These creatures help pollinate over 90 species of crops that you eat.

To attract pollinators like bees, flowers are often brightly colored.

Pollen sticks to the bee's legs and fuzzy body.

How pollination works

Pollination is the way flowering plants reproduce. When a pollinator like a bee visits a flower, it accidentally picks up some pollen. When it visits another flower, it accidentally delivers the pollen. If pollen makes it from one flower's **anther** to another flower's **pistil**, its seeds will be fertilized—ready to turn into new plants.

The bee picks up pollen from the anther.

Then the bee delivers the pollen to the pistil of another plant.

The Honeyguide and the Humans

A type of African bird, called a honeyguide, makes a great team with humans. Honeyguides lead humans to beehives. Then humans get rid of the bees, so they can both enjoy the honey. Some scientists think this partnership dates back almost two million years!

Honey hunters

To work together, these species first need to find each other. Either party can initiate: A bird can find honey and then tell a human about it, or a human can get hungry and find a bird to help them search.

This way!

Honeyguides show the humans where to go by flying toward the beehive, stopping, calling out, and waiting for the humans to reply, before repeating the process.

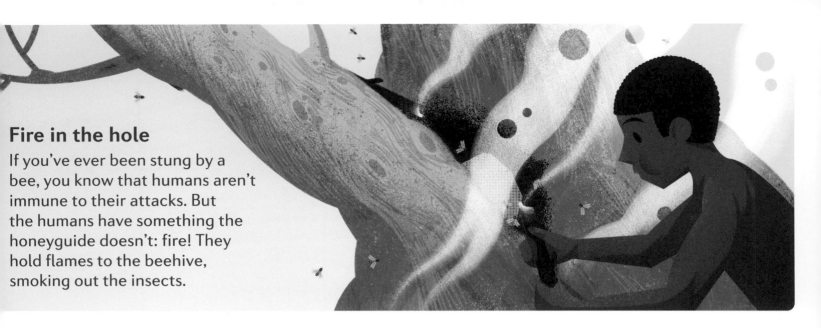

Fire in the hole

If you've ever been stung by a bee, you know that humans aren't immune to their attacks. But the humans have something the honeyguide doesn't: fire! They hold flames to the beehive, smoking out the insects.

Sharing the spoils

The humans are fair to their honeyguide friend—once they've secured some honeycomb, they break it up and toss some to their avian assistant. No wonder they've been colleagues for so long!

The Spider Crab
and the Algae

Japanese spider crabs aren't anything like the crabs you find on the beach. Their legs can be enormously long, up to 13 ft (4 m) from end to end, and they live up to 2,000 ft (610 m) underneath the sea! Dangerous predators stalk them through the depths, but they have a secret weapon: **camouflage**. This is the ability to cleverly blend into their surroundings.

Naked and afraid

Without a disguise to protect it, a Japanese spider crab is a painfully obvious prey item. Its bright red body stands out like a sore thumb against the muted colors of the seabed.

Hidden crab

In the military, a "ghillie suit" is an outfit soldiers wear if they want to hide. It's often made with leaves and branches from the local area. Japanese spider crabs do exactly the same thing—except they use algae! Covered in these tiny plants, the crabs are almost invisible on top of algae-covered rock. The crab gets an invisibility cloak to keep it safe from hungry predators such as octopuses, while the algae get a mobile home.

The Capybara and the

Capybaras can weigh as much as a fridge!

Cattle Tyrant

The capybara may be the largest rodent on Earth, but these goliaths need protection from a swarm of mini monsters. Tiny horseflies try to suck capybara blood, and the only thing stopping them is the cattle tyrant—a tough, insect-hunting bird. From the cattle tyrant's perspective, the capybara is the perfect bait for its fly prey.

The enemy

The sworn enemy of the capybara and the natural prey of the cattle tyrant, horseflies navigate through a hailstorm of beaks to get to the capybara's blood.

River swimmers

The capybara may look like a supersized guinea pig, but these beasts are expert swimmers. They can hold their breath for up to five minutes!

The Humpback Whale
and the Barnacles

Upon landing on a whale, barnacles crawl toward the mouth, where they form large colonies.

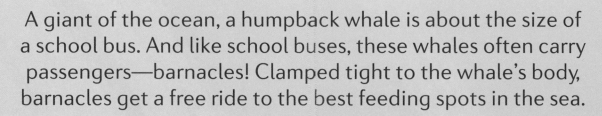

A giant of the ocean, a humpback whale is about the size of a school bus. And like school buses, these whales often carry passengers—barnacles! Clamped tight to the whale's body, barnacles get a free ride to the best feeding spots in the sea.

Barnacles start off as tiny swimming larvae. Scientists aren't sure how they manage to hitch a ride on a whale.

Barnacles dig into the whale's skin and form a hard shell.

What's in it for me?

As the whale swims, the barnacles stick out feathery filaments to catch small organisms called plankton. It isn't clear what the humpback gets from the relationship. The barnacles might even slow it down.

The Ants and the Fungus

Leaf-cutter ants practically invented civilization before humans. These tiny critters live in complex colonies containing up to eight million individuals. Their cities are complete with rooms, tunnels, roads—and fungus farms! Growing fungus for the ants to eat is a team effort, and everyone in the colony is involved.

On the march

To grow fungus the ants first need to gather leaves. The ants can decimate a tree in a matter of hours. They tirelessly climb up and down its branches, cutting off as many leaves as they can carry.

Chambers

The ants live in giant cities that host up to 2,000 separate chambers with different functions.

Her highness

The founder of this whole operation—the queen—sits tucked away in her quarters, producing the millions of eggs that will become the ants who serve her.

All roads lead to the colony

These ants build roads. They clear paths to and from their home, keeping them clear and guarding them against predators. The roads make it easier to bring leaves home.

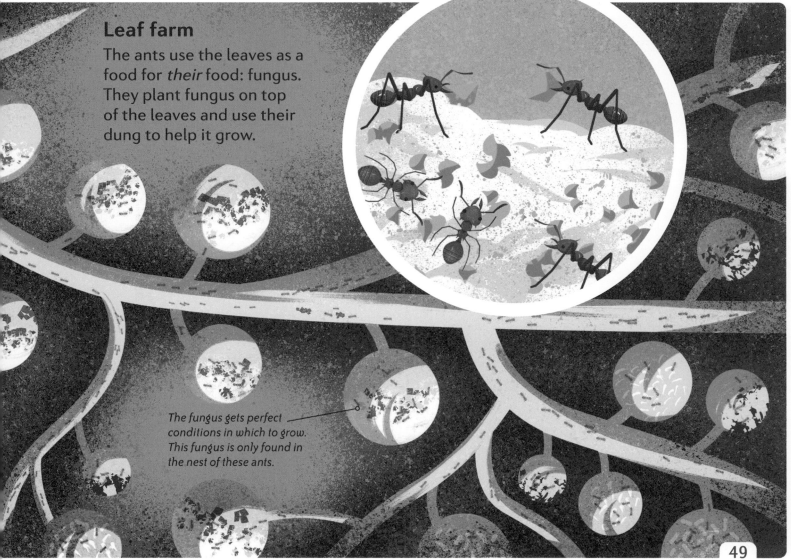

Leaf farm

The ants use the leaves as a food for *their* food: fungus. They plant fungus on top of the leaves and use their dung to help it grow.

The fungus gets perfect conditions in which to grow. This fungus is only found in the nest of these ants.

The Crayfish and the Worms

The crayfish is more than an animal—it's a whole habitat! On its body, in its gills, and even in its wounds there are colonies of tiny worms known as branchiobdellida (good luck pronouncing that). The worms get food and shelter, but do they give anything back? Scientists aren't sure. Let's take a look at the evidence.

Take a deep breath

The gills of a crayfish, which it uses to breathe, are perfect homes for the worms. Some scientists think the worms eat tiny organisms and debris inside the gills, clearing them up and allowing the crayfish to breathe easier.

Water leaves gills

Water enters gills

Mini worms

Meet branchiobdellida: tiny worms who can't survive without a crayfish. These little creatures are closely related to leeches. The illustration on the left shows one much bigger than they are in real life—some of them are smaller than the period at the end of this sentence.

Wounded animal

Other researchers note that the worms enjoy living inside the open wounds of crayfish. Sometimes they feed on the crayfish's flesh, which makes it harder for the wound to heal. Do you think the worms are good or bad for their crayfish hosts?

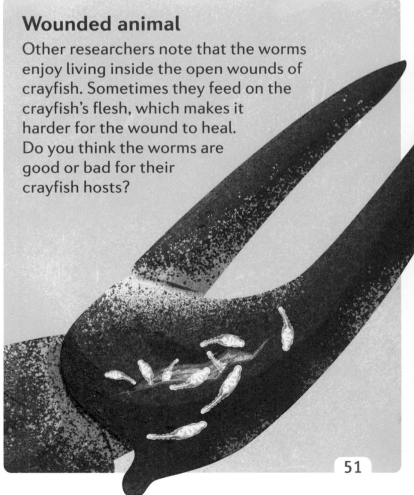

The Elephant Shrew and the Lily

The elephant shrew, a small mammal from Africa, shares a special relationship with the pagoda lily plant. The elephant shrew is the lily's adorable pollinator-in-chief, and the lily is the provider of the elephant shrew's favorite food in the whole wide world.

Shrew or elephant?

The elephant shrew got its name because its long nose reminded people of an elephant's trunk. Coincidentally, scientists later found out that this shrewlike creature isn't a shrew at all— it's actually more closely related to elephants!

Fair exchange

When the elephant shrew reaches in for its favorite treat—pagoda lily nectar—it gets pollen on its nose. The elephant shrew carries the pollen to the next plant it visits, in the process pollinating the plant so it can produce seeds. This means both mammal and plant benefit from the relationship.

The best item on the menu

Scientists have tried to find a food that the elephant shrew prefers. They offered it water, peanut butter, and apples, but it always went for the pagoda lily.

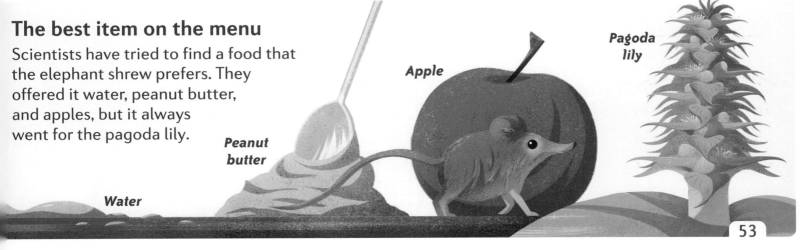

Water

Peanut butter

Apple

Pagoda lily

The Giant Tube Worm and the Bacteria

At the bottom of the ocean, so deep no sunlight can reach them, two alien-like creatures rely on each other to get a good meal. The freaky-looking giant tube worm doesn't have a mouth or any way to digest food, so it works with tiny living things called bacteria—who live inside it—to create the energy they both need to survive.

The worms grow near boiling hot hydrothermal vents on the seabed. They're heated by the center of the Earth and provide the nutrients the bacteria need to eat.

Eating for two

The giant tube worm uses its plume to collect nourishing nutrients from the ocean. It then sends them to the bacteria, which in turn create food for the worm. The bacteria get a place to grow and reproduce with constant meals!

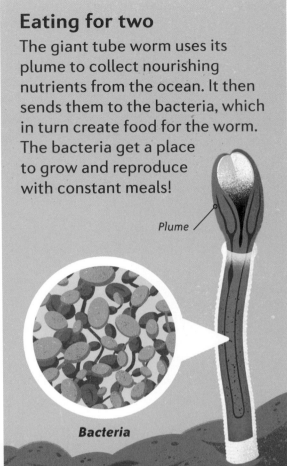

Plume

Bacteria

Healthy diet

The bacteria are doing a great job. The worms can grow to the height of a basketball hoop!

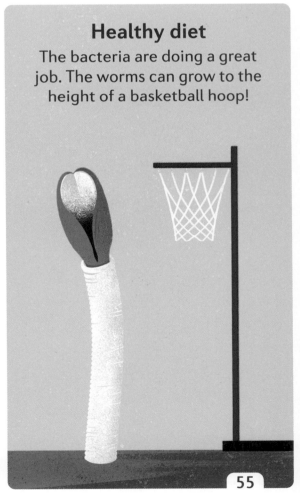

The Human and the Head Lice

Warning: reading this page *will* make your head itchy! Head lice are tiny insects that evolved to feed on human blood. They lay eggs, also known as nits, in your hair and suck blood straight from your scalp. This illustration may look like a dense jungle, but those "trees" are actually hairs! If you have lice, this is what a close-up of your scalp looks like.

As many as **one in ten** kids have **head lice**.

Head lice don't have wings, and they can't jump. That means they rely on you to accidentally pick them up from someone else.

Even a big nit is smaller than a grain of sand. Good luck finding it!

The Grouper and the Octopus

This duo may not look like they'd be friends, but the octopus and a fish called the grouper discovered a mutual interest. Both animals love to eat fish, and on this sliver of common ground a fearsome hunting party was born.

1. Out and about

The octopus and the grouper cruise the neighborhood, scouring the seafloor for potential prey.

2. Check this out

The grouper spots a fish hiding in the reef and tells the octopus by turning its body into an arrow. It points its nose directly at the desired victim.

3. Flush 'em out

The grouper may have figured out how to
point without arms, but it can't reach into
crevices without the help of its octopus friend.
The octopus reaches its tentacles into every
entrance in the reef until the fish is scared
out of hiding. Dinner is served for the
one who can catch it first!

59

The Woolly Bat and the Pitcher Plant

Pitcher plants originally evolved to trap, kill, and digest unsuspecting animals. They're a type of **carnivorous** (meat-eating) plant that attracts prey with a sweet scent and then drowns it in digestive fluids. But this particular species has evolved a more peaceful strategy—and it's all to do with a sleepy bat.

Time for a snooze

Most pitcher plants hope to use the promise of sweet nectar to lure in their prey, but this one uses a good night's sleep. This plant offers a comfortable roost, just the right size for its bat friend to nap comfortably.

Bed and breakfast

The bat poops in its sleep (yes, really) and its droppings fall into the plant's digestive fluids. This might seem like a bad meal, but it gives the pitcher plant the essential nutrients it needs to grow. Bed for the bat, breakfast for the plant!

Bat poop

The sea is full of floating food for the urchin to eat while it's carried around.

Predators see the spines and decide not to bother attacking the crab.

Carrier crabs stand on their front four legs and carry with the back four. (It's the crab equivalent of a handstand.)

The Carrier Crab and the Urchin

Do you have a hat you really love? One you want to wear everywhere? Well, for the carrier crab the hat of choice is a sea urchin. It is the carrier crab's only defense against the dangers of the deep. By carrying around a spiny, venomous animal above its head, the crab guarantees predators won't try to attack it. But the crab may not be the only one who benefits from this unusual arrangement—the urchin uses the crab as a form of transportation, riding it like a horse.

Safe travels
On occasion, little fish have been witnessed swimming in and around the spines of an urchin as it's carried by a crab. These fish have lucked out—they get all the protection of the urchin's spines, without having to carry the urchin!

The Zebra
and the
Wildebeest

The zebra mows down the tall parts of the grass...

Every year, over a million wildebeest and hundreds of thousands of zebras travel between the African countries Tanzania and Kenya in search of food. On this journey, the zebra and the wildebeest are frequent travel buddies. Despite feeding on the same grasses, these two aren't competitors—they're each after a different part of the grass. The zebra goes high, while the wildebeest goes low!

...and the wildebeest eats what's left.

65

The Cuckoo and the Reed Warbler

The crafty cuckoo lays her eggs in the nests of other birds, such as reed warblers, forcing them to raise her chicks as their own. It's parenthood without the responsibility!

1. Scare tactics

First, the cuckoo pretends to be a predator to scare a reed warbler away from its nest.

2. Bad egg

The cuckoo lays her egg in the abandoned nest. The egg looks a bit like a reed warbler's—this makes it less likely to notice the new addition.

3. Sibling rivalry

The cuckoo egg hatches earlier than the reed warbler eggs. The young cuckoo pushes the other eggs out to make sure it gets all of its adoptive parents' attention.

Master of disguise

An adult cuckoo is a relatively harmless bird, but it has a terrifying costume. Its banded underbelly helps it resemble a sparrowhawk—a natural predator to birds like reed warblers.

Cuckoo

Sparrowhawk

4. Big baby

The cuckoo baby is steadily fed by both reed warbler parents. By stealing a nest's worth of food, it grows to an enormous size—often much bigger than its adoptive parents. Mother cuckoo's plan was a success, and she didn't have to lift a finger (or rather, a wing!).

Hummingbirds can visit thousands of flowers every day.

The Hummingbirds and the Flowers

Hummingbirds not only can hover, they can also fly backward.

Tiny bird

The smallest bird on the planet is the bee hummingbird. Fully grown it is barely 2 in (5 cm) long. It could comfortably perch on a pencil!

This illustration is life-size!

The tongue for the task

The hummingbird's long beak and longer tongue are tremendous assets. They allow the hummingbird to reach into flowers and pump nectar down its throat. It drinks nectar at a rate of 14 licks per second—these birds do everything fast.

Some hummingbirds flap their wings 80 times per second!

Hummingbirds are the bees of the bird world. These pollinators hover from flower to flower, consuming nectar with their straw-like tongues. Along the way they pick up pollen, before distributing it to other flowers they visit. The flowers do their best to attract hummingbirds with bright colors and sugary nectar.

Some hummingbirds have tongues longer than their bodies. When the tongue is not in use, it curls up inside the hummingbird's head.

The Eel and the Wrasse

The moray eel is perhaps the most vicious predator on the reef—and yet, here it is, letting tiny fish enter and leave its mouth unharmed. Why does it show mercy? And *what* are these little cleaner wrasses *thinking*? Well, these fish have set up an eel-washing business. The cleaner wrasses eat the eel's parasites until it's spotless. The eel gets clean, the cleaner wrasses get fed.

The false cleanerfish evolved to look like a cleaner wrasse to avoid being eaten!

Disloyal customer

As much as the moray eel enjoys the help of the cleaner wrasse, it has no loyalty. If another kind of animal—such as a cleaner shrimp—is willing to do the same job for the same price, the moray eel will accept its business without a second thought.

The Warthog and the Mongooses

Warthogs have a problem: They're covered in tiny, itchy, bloodsucking, disease-carrying ticks! Their cloven hooves and enormous tusks don't allow them to remove bugs by themselves. Instead, they visit mongooses, the best bug-busters in Africa. All a warthog needs to do is lie down and the mongooses will do the rest, scouring the warthog's skin until they've eaten every last insect. This treatment is quite relaxing—sometimes, the warthog falls asleep. The mongooses get a free snack, and the warthog gets some nice pampering.

The Leafflower Moth and the Tree

1. Sweet smells

First, the leafflower tree's flowers lure in a female leafflower moth with a sweet scent.

2. Collecting pollen

When the moth lands to feed on sugary nectar, she collects pollen. She'll take this to other flowers and pollinate them.

3. Laying an egg

When the moth finds a suitable flower, she lays an egg in it. The flower then grows into a fruit, with the egg inside it!

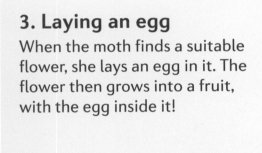

4. Metamorphosis

The egg hatches inside the fruit and the caterpillar eats some seeds. Then it begins to **metamorphose**—a process that turns it into an adult moth.

5. All grown up

The leafflower moth spends most of its first year on Earth inside the fruit, patiently waiting for its moment to join the wider world.

This partnership is pollination—with a twist! The leafflower moth pollinates the leafflower tree, but unlike most other pollinators in this book, it gets a whole lot more than food out of the deal...

Fully grown, free, and ready to repeat the cycle!

The fruit opens in March.

6. Leaving home

Finally, after months of the moth being trapped inside, the fruit ripens and opens up. The moth flies free!

The Vampire Bats and the Pigs

Vampire bats, true to their name, live on the blood of other animals. In the last few thousand years, farm animals have become their favorite food. Bred by humans to be large, slow, and defenseless—and kept all in one handy place—pigs have become the ideal prey for vampire bats. They sneak in at night and steal blood from sleeping hogs.

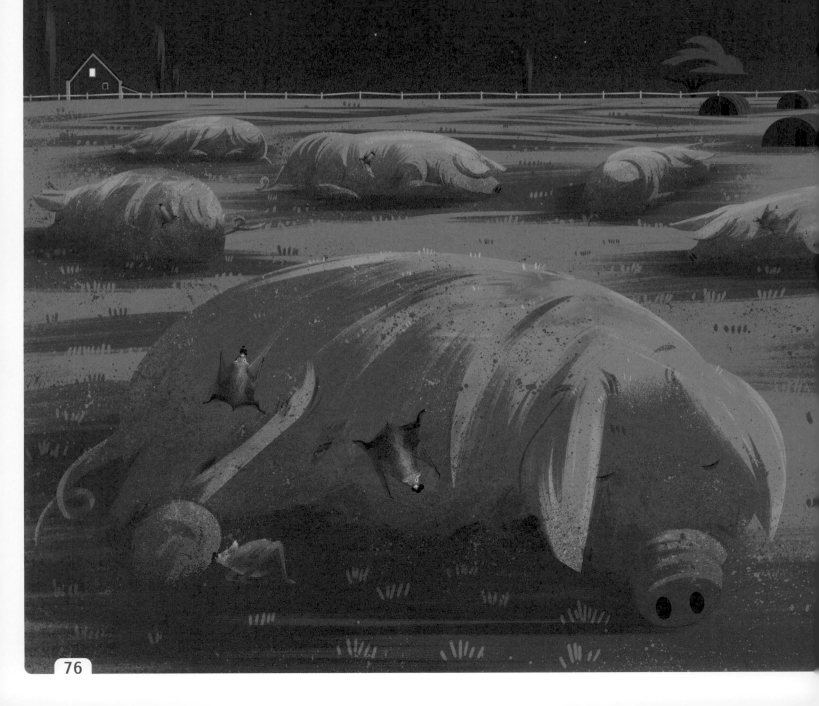

Count Dracula or Robin Hood?

You wouldn't think vampires would be generous, but these ones are! If a vampire bat notices that another is looking a little skinny, it will often regurgitate (bring back up) some blood for its friend.

I want to suck your blood!

Well, not exactly. Rather than sucking the blood out of its victims, the vampire bat makes a small cut using its razor-sharp teeth, and then uses its tongue to lap up the blood.

The Mosquito and the Orchid

You might think of the mosquito only as a pest—a miniature vampire determined to ruin every stroll through the woods. However, when it isn't buzzing in your ear, the snow pool mosquito spends its time pollinating plants, such as the blunt-leaved orchid.

Nice guys

Mosquitoes have a bad reputation for spreading disease, but when it comes to bloodsucking they're not always as bad as they seem. Female mosquitoes only rarely drink blood, and then only to feed their young. Male mosquitoes, meanwhile, don't drink any blood at all.

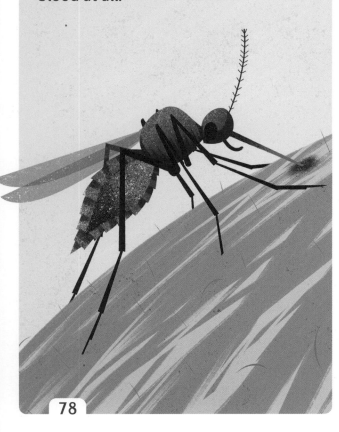

Orchid perfume

Snow pool mosquitoes aren't the pickiest eaters, but they *do* have a favorite food. When they smell a blunt-leaved orchid, they're drawn to the scent like moths to a light!

Pollen hats

These orchids evolved a funny way of making pollination more effective. The flowers are shaped so that if mosquitoes lean in for some nectar, a dollop of pollen will fall right on their heads. They look like they're wearing tiny little hats! Who knew mosquitoes could be so cute?

When the mosquitoes duck their heads into flowers, the pollen on their hats rubs off, pollinating the plant.

The Manta Ray and the Remoras

With gigantic wings, the manta ray is like an underwater jet. This passenger plane of a sea creature soars through the ocean with a whole host of passengers, called remoras, on board. As well as a free ride, these fish are eager to see the in-flight meal—they fill themselves up on parasites that fall off the manta ray's skin.

Fasten your seatbelts

The remora's head acts like a suction cup. It presses its flat head against the manta ray, sticking the two together in a similar way to a bath toy that sticks to the side of the tub. Scientists used the remora as inspiration to make a super sticky robot!

Some scientists think **manta rays** can recognize themselves in a **mirror**.

The Birds and the Trees

In the bird world, trees are building sites and construction materials wrapped into one. Most of the world's birds build their nests *in* trees, using stuff they get *from* trees. Trees would do just fine without birds, but most bird species rely on their wooden friends.

Woven home

Baya weavers knit their nests from grass and hang them from branches. The males make these to impress their girlfriends!

Tiny nest

If you've read pages 68–69, it probably won't surprise you to find out that the smallest nest in the world is built by the tiniest bird in the world—the bee hummingbird! The nest is only 1 in (3 cm) wide.

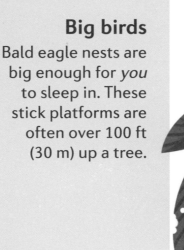

Big birds

Bald eagle nests are big enough for *you* to sleep in. These stick platforms are often over 100 ft (30 m) up a tree.

Bird apartments

This is the closest thing in nature to an apartment building. Up to 100 social weaver birds work together to build a multiunit nest, divided into two-room homes for each couple.

Just one of this building's many tenants.

Ovenbird

The rufous hornero, a type of ovenbird, carefully crafts a nest out of mud and manure. Once complete it leaves the nest to dry hard in the sun like clay.

Common tailorbird

The baya weaver likes knitting, but the common tailorbird prefers sewing. This creature stitches together a leaf nest using spiderwebs as its thread.

The Large Blue and the Red Ant

The large blue butterfly manages to trick an entire ant colony into raising her young for her. Read carefully if you want to understand her plan—this insect is a mastermind!

1. Ant poison

It starts when a wild thyme plant is under attack by an underground red ant colony. It releases a chemical distress signal.

2. The plot

The butterfly smells the distress signal and knows there is an ant colony underneath the wild thyme plant. She lays an egg on it.

3. Enter the caterpillar

The egg hatches. The resulting caterpillar fattens up on wild thyme leaves before dropping to the ground and curling up like a grub in the dirt.

4. Mistaken identity

Eventually, a local ant comes along and mistakes the little caterpillar for one of its youngsters, or larvae. It assumes the grub has somehow escaped from the colony. It takes the caterpillar to its home and into the nesting chamber. The large blue's trick has worked! At this point, the caterpillar also produces a droplet of sweet liquid, which the ant drinks.

5. The traitor

Once inside, the caterpillar starts clucking—imitating the ants' queen to gain their trust. At the same time, the caterpillar begins eating the ants' actual larvae! (The ants don't think much of this cannibalism—real queens sometimes eat their offspring.)

6. Mission complete

The caterpillar grows to 50 times its original size before turning into a butterfly. Then it spreads its wings and flies off, sniffing for another distress signal, hoping to repeat the cycle.

The Pack Rat and the Pseudoscorpion

The pack rat frolics around the wilds of North America with a tiny freeloader—the pseudoscorpion—on its back. Many scientists believe this is a form of **commensalism**, where one animal (the pseudoscorpion) benefits, while the other (the pack rat) doesn't benefit but isn't harmed either.

Little passenger
The pseudoscorpion is barely bigger than a couple of grains of sand. At that size, it can't travel far alone, so it hitches a ride on the pack rat. It has been suggested that the pseudoscorpion pays its travel fare by eating parasites.

Roommates

Not only does the pseudoscorpion get a free ride, it also gets a sweet place to live! The pack rat often takes its rider back home, sheltering it from harsh weather and dangerous predators.

Terrible taste

Pack rats take home more than just pseudoscorpions. They like to decorate their nests, and sometimes they grab our trash and treat it like a treasure. These small rodents are especially enchanted by shiny stuff, such as aluminum foil.

The Wolves
and the Hyena

A classic clue

Scientists confirmed this relationship when they found hyena and wolf footprints together. The researchers knew the different species were walking in a pack because the footprints overlapped.

This relationship is the most mysterious in the book. Only two pieces of evidence prove it exists, and nobody knows its nature. All we know is that these two predators—hyenas and wolves—have lived in harmony at least once. Scientists in Israel documented a single hyena living in a pack of wolves. Why they teamed up and how they helped each other remains unknown.

One-time thing?

This relationship has only been witnessed once. It's possible that the tracks and the sighting are both of the same specific friendship. These two species might never have worked together before and may never do so again...

89

The Crab Spiders and the Flowers

Different types of crab spider have evolved to blend in *perfectly* with different colored flowers. They lie in wait for insects to visit, and then ambush them. At first glance, this hardly looks like friendship—it looks like the crab spiders are sabotaging one of the most positive relationships in nature! How is a flower meant to reproduce if a spider is attacking all the pollinators? But before we judge, let's take a closer look.

Not helpful

Sometimes, a crab spider takes out bees while they're pollinating flowers. Admittedly, this is a loss for everybody except the spider. The bee dies, and the flower doesn't get pollinated—only the spider gets fed.

Sound the alarm!

Oh no! A caterpillar is eating the petals of the flower, threatening to severely damage the plant. Where is a crab spider when you need one? The flower releases a chemical alarm as a cry for help.

The crab spider's redemption

A nearby crab spider detects that the flower is in danger—the flower's alarm bell is the spider's dinner bell. The spider climbs the plant and eats the caterpillar, preventing any further damage. Crab spider to the rescue!

The **Human** and the **Dogs**

Earning their keep

In the past, dogs were mostly working animals. They were used for things like hunting or pulling sleds. Though dogs were given food and shelter, humans got the better deal. From an evolutionary perspective, this relationship was **mutualistic**, meaning that by working together both species improved their chance to survive and reproduce.

Once upon a time dogs, evolved from wild wolves. For thousands of years they have worked closely with humans, but over time the relationship between the two species has changed. Dogs have gone from hard workers to pampered pooches.

Parasitic pets

You might not group your furry friend with parasites like leeches and mosquitoes, but these days dogs take from humans without giving anything back. (From an evolutionary perspective—we're not counting licks and cuddles.) This relationship is therefore **parasitic**. Dogs get help surviving and reproducing, and humans pay for it.

The Ants and the Acacia

Ants act as the bullhorn acacia tree's security system. The acacia houses and feeds them, and in its time of need the ants will rise to defend it—attacking any who dare threaten their beloved tree. Instead of evolving the ability to protect itself, this tree evolved to attract others who can!

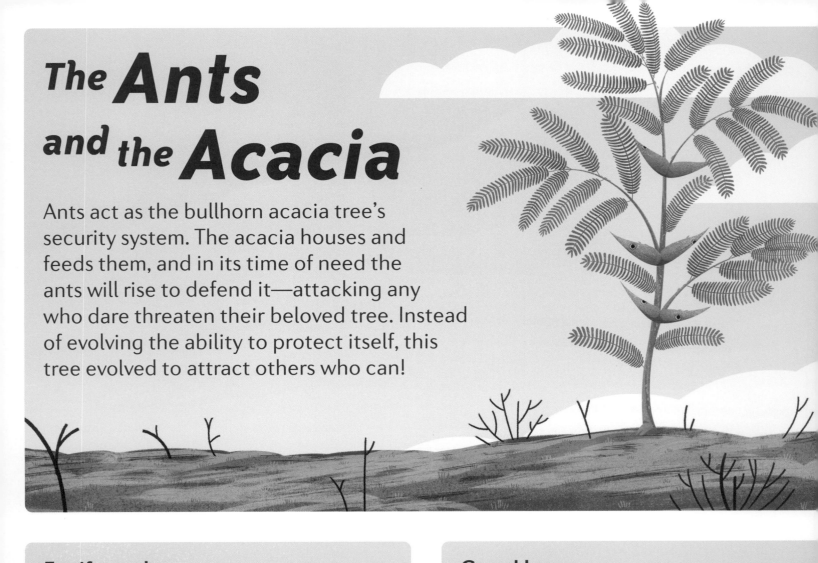

Eat if you dare

Many creatures try to eat the acacia's tasty leaves—and many come to regret it. No matter how big the threat, the ants will give everything they can, biting the enemy ferociously until it decides to give up.

Guard bugs

These ants are more than happy to pick on someone their own size, too. If a hungry caterpillar crawls on their precious plant, they'll happily teach it not to trespass.

Energy drink

Defending a tree is thirsty work. Luckily for the ants, the tree is always oozing nectar, nature's sugary energy drink.

Beltian bodies

The tree pays the ants with something it evolved especially for them: Beltian bodies. These delicious packets of fat and protein grow from the tip of each leaf for the ants to eat.

Living quarters

Acacia ants live inside the enormous thorns of the acacia tree. This means off-duty guards (and their babies) can stay safe from danger. You couldn't think of a more appropriate home for these feisty insects.

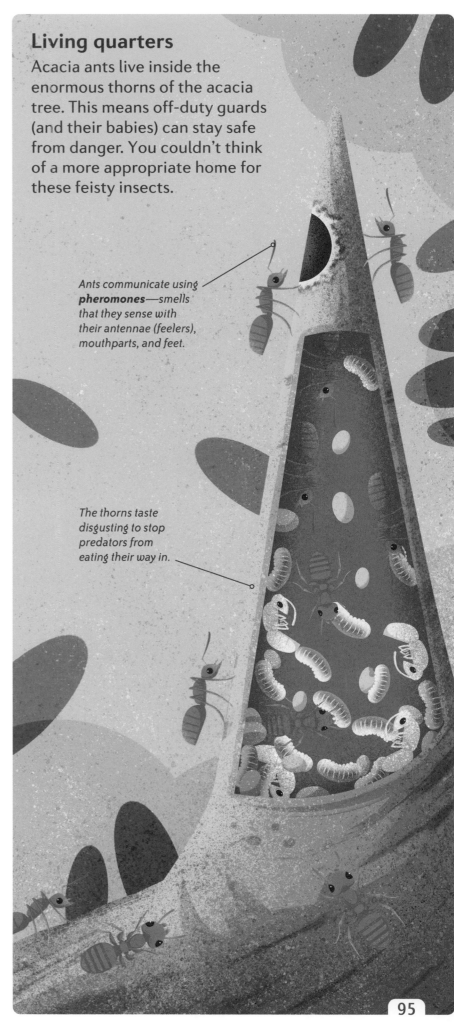

Ants communicate using **pheromones**—smells that they sense with their antennae (feelers), mouthparts, and feet.

The thorns taste disgusting to stop predators from eating their way in.

The Woodpeckers and the Cactus

Inhospitable home

The reasons you wouldn't want to live in a cactus are the same reasons the Gila woodpeckers can't wait to move in. The spines aren't particularly inviting, but the woodpeckers don't want company—they're delighted to live in a thorny fortress where predators can't get their precious eggs.

Bug hunters

The woodpecker couple do substantial damage to the saguaro cactus when they move in—they peck a hole in the cactus's side. However, they protect the cactus from a far worse fate. Bugs are constantly threatening to infest the cactus, but the critters make a perfect woodpecker snack.

You might imagine that a cactus wouldn't want
bird renters—its spines are the ultimate "no vacancy" sign.
While having woodpeckers move in does damage
the cactus, the birds pay their rent with the best
exterminator services in the desert.

The Human and the Corn

Before humans got our hands on it, corn (also known as maize) was nothing special. It was a small grassy plant limited to Central America. Now, mere thousands of years after we started farming it, it's one of the most successful plant species on Earth! Corn has spread to other parts of North America, Africa, Asia, South America, and Europe, and it covers over 350 million acres worldwide.

In it for ourselves

Of course, humans didn't help corn achieve world domination for its own sake. We plant corn around the world so we can use it for all sorts of things—including feeding it to farm animals, turning it into fuel, and eating it as corn on the cob and breakfast cereal!

Humans invented machines, such as combine harvesters, to help them pick corn.

99

The Squirrel and the Oak Tree

Everybody knows squirrels love acorns, but acorns love squirrels too! Squirrels like to bury acorns in secret locations to stock up for the winter—they're the perfect emergency snack. However, squirrels only remember where they put *some* of their acorns, so they accidentally plant a lot of oak trees.

Saved for later

In fall, squirrels collect tasty acorns from oak trees. They bury the acorns all over the place, knowing that they'll need them when winter comes and there isn't much to eat.

Glad you forgot!

When winter arrives, the squirrels don't always remember where they put their food. Squirrels forget to recover up to 74% of their acorns! (Considering they bury thousands of them, it's actually pretty impressive they remember so many.)

The circle of life

Next year, a forgotten acorn will have turned into a young oak tree. When it matures, it will support the local squirrels for hundreds of years. They will, in turn, plant more trees with their forgetfulness.

The Tortoise and the Beetle

This North American tortoise is lucky enough to have a live-in maid. A little beetle resides in the gopher tortoise's den and eats its poop! Sounds strange, but it's a great deal for both parties: The gopher tortoise doesn't have to worry about stepping in its own poop or parasites living in the old dung. Meanwhile the beetle gets a delicious meal (well, it thinks so). While these two animals have a special relationship, it isn't entirely unique—the gopher tortoise also benefits hundreds of other species thanks to its impressive den.

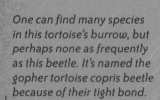

One can find many species in this tortoise's burrow, but perhaps none as frequently as this beetle. It's named the gopher tortoise copris beetle because of their tight bond.

Welcome at the inn

Because the gopher tortoise digs such awesome burrows, animals of all kinds want to move in. This tortoise has been found living with hundreds of species, including snakes, skunks, frogs, and even owls!

Florida burrowing owl

Cricket

Gopher frog

Though gopher tortoises rarely measure over 1 ft (30 cm), they can dig holes 5 ft (4.5 m) long!

Wolf spider

Indigo snake

Skunk

The Sloth and the Algae

The sloth on the right may look like it has dyed its hair green, but really, it's just covered in tiny plants known as algae. The sloth's fur is sheltered, warm, moist, and full of nutrients, making it an ideal greenhouse in which the algae can grow. And there's a benefit for the sloth, too—algae provides awesome camouflage, helping the furry mammal blend into the trees and stay safe from predators.

A sloth's natural color stands out more among branches and leaves.

As well as algae, a type of moth sometimes lives in sloth fur. It feeds on the algae, and its young eat sloth poop!

Tasty snack

Algae might be the world's only edible disguise. Any time an algae-covered sloth gets hungry, it can pick some out of its fur and enjoy a little snack. This means the algae help the sloth eat *and* avoid being eaten!

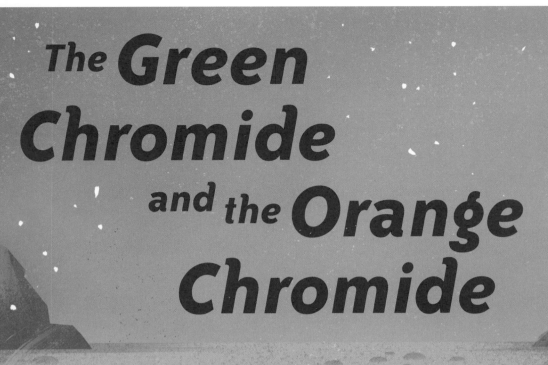

The Green Chromide and the Orange Chromide

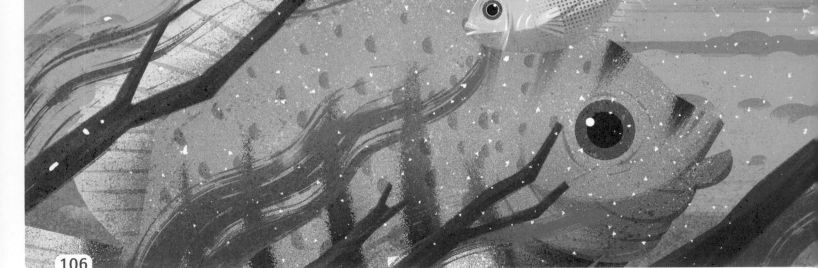

This is a not-so-friendly, not-so-simple spin on a cleaning partnership. The orange chromide fish eats parasites off the much larger green chromide. This benefits the green chromide by reducing the number of parasites it has to cope with, and it secures the orange chromide a meal. But there's a twist: If a green chromide leaves its eggs unattended, the orange chromide will eat them without a moment's hesitation!

Traitor

These two species could have had a peaceful, mutually beneficial friendship. But the orange chromide has no sense of loyalty—so it eats its client's unborn babies.

The Lemur and the Palm

A big plant needs a big pollinator, and at 4 ft (1.2 m) long, the black-and-white ruffed lemur is the largest pollinator in the world. It scales the massive traveler's palm, opens its flowers, and drinks the sweet nectar inside. While it feeds, the lemur's long fur mops up plenty of pollen. It takes this to the next palm, fertilizing its seeds and allowing more palms to grow.

The **traveler's palm** can grow taller than an **Olympic diving board**.

Breaking...

Forget the dainty flowers you're used to—these flowers are fortresses. This lemur is the only pollinator capable of getting to the nectar inside them.

...and entering

Once it has managed to push its way in, the lemur sticks its face straight into the plant, lapping up as much nectar as it can get.

Messy eater

While it drinks, the lemur picks up a whole lot of pollen on its face. Its dense fur makes it an excellent pollinator—a little like a massive bumblebee.

Blue seeds

As if the traveler's palm wasn't already absurd-looking enough, its seeds are bright blue! This may help the plant attract lemurs, who can only see blues and greens.

The Lemon Ants

The Amazon rainforest is famed for its amazing number of different plants, but in some areas only certain species of tree survive. Local legends say these creepy dead zones, called "devil's gardens," are created by an evil spirit—in truth, they are cultivated by lemon ants.

Happy forest
Before the little ants come along, the Amazon rainforest is a tropical paradise. All manner of beautiful plants grow alongside one another.

and the Devil's Garden

Happy ants

However, the lemon ants only want to live on certain kinds of tree. They inject a natural plant killer (called a **herbicide**) into every other type of plant in the area to make more space for their favorite species. This results in stretches of forest that are eerily empty, except for the ants and their favorite trees.

The Cowbird and the Yellowthroat

The brown-headed cowbird is often called the "mafia bird" because of its habit of forcing other birds to raise its young. It lays eggs in the nests of other bird species, such as the yellowthroat, and comes back to check its offspring are being well cared for.

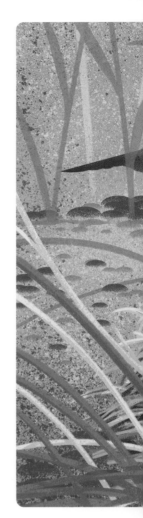

Mafia bird

Members of the Mafia are famous for carrying out extortion rackets. Basically: pay a fee or suffer the consequences. In essence, this bird does the same thing.

Cooperate...

If the yellowthroat agrees to raise the cowbird's chick, it's paid a hefty fee. Raising your own kids is costly enough, but raising the young of another species is a complete waste of time from an evolutionary standpoint.

...or else!

If the yellowthroat destroys, neglects, or removes the cowbird's egg, revenge will be swift and merciless. The cowbird will come back, discover what has happened, and smash all of the yellowthroat's own eggs.

The Boxer Crab and the Anemones

Most boxing gloves keep opponents safer—but the boxer crab's gloves put its enemies in great danger. It carries a pair of venomous anemones, and if a predator gets too close, it will throw a stinging blow straight to the face. These anemones help the crab defeat much bigger predators, truly punching above its weight.

Put 'em up

The anemones let this crab pack a venomous punch: If a predator so much as touches their tentacles, they'll launch venomous barbs straight into its flesh. Usually, merely raising the gloves is enough to make a threat back down.

Friend or hostage?

Some think the anemones benefit from being carried, through free safety and transportation. Others believe the crab stunts the anemones' growth by stealing their food.

Attack of the clones

Scientists tested the information contained in the DNA of the crab's anemones and found that each pair usually shared a 100% match with each other. They concluded that the boxer crab must start with only one anemone but "clone" it by ripping it in half and letting each side regrow.

The Swift Parrot and the Blue Gum

The swift parrot and the blue gum tree would struggle to reproduce without each other's help. Every year, swift parrots return to the Australian island of Tasmania to breed, and while they're there, they help the blue gum trees breed too. The birds nest in the trees and survive on their sweet, sugary nectar, but they end up covered in pollen whenever they eat. They carry this pollen from tree to tree, fertilizing seeds at every stop.

The blue gum flower evolved to satisfy the swift parrot's taste buds.

Off to the races

The swift parrot flies at highway speeds. "Swift" is right—this is the fastest parrot on the planet. It can top 55 miles per hour (88 km per hour). That's faster than a racehorse!

Breeding season

All swift parrots are born in Tasmania, but they spend most of their lives in mainland Australia. They return to Tasmania only to breed. The ocean crossing is over 500 miles (800 km), so this bird has endurance as well as speed.

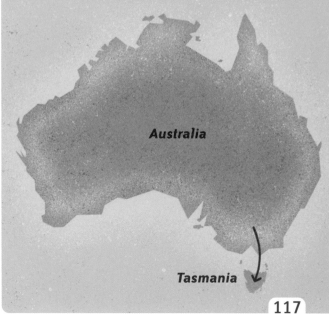

Australia

Tasmania

The Pilot Fish
and the Great White

Cleaning crew

Tiny parasites can do serious harm to a shark, so the pilot fish provide a tremendous service. The shark gets a fleet of personal assistants, and the pilot fish get a source of regular meals—the parasites on one shark can sustain a whole school of pilot fish.

Most sea creatures are wise to steer clear of the great white shark. However, it's perfectly friendly to a select few creatures, including pilot fish. Pilot fish avoid becoming shark food not by fleeing or fighting back, but by nibbling irritating parasites off the shark's body.

Great white sharks are the largest meat-eating fish.

The Drongo and the Meerkats

The drongo is the local lookout bird. Whenever it sees a predator on the horizon, the neighborhood drongo sounds the alarm and everybody runs for cover. But the drongo often takes advantage of the community's trust, abusing it for personal gain...

Watch out!

When the drongo sees a predator, it lets out a distinct call to warn its meerkat friends. Meerkats listen for these calls to get a heads-up whenever danger is incoming.

The lie

The drongo *knows* the meerkats are listening, and so sometimes it makes a fake alarm call to scare the meerkats away. Who knew birds could lie?

The motive

The drongo tricks the meerkats for a cheap meal. When it sees a meerkat eating a tasty treat (such as a scorpion), it can frighten it away with its fake call and take the food for itself.

The Goby and the Shrimp

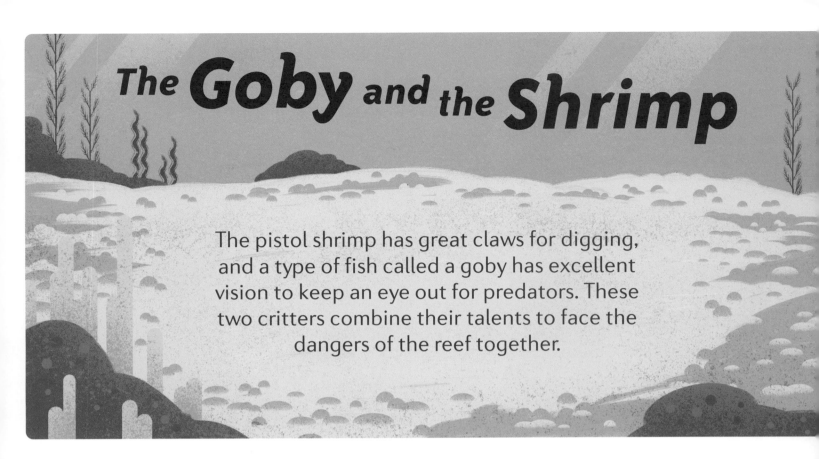

The pistol shrimp has great claws for digging, and a type of fish called a goby has excellent vision to keep an eye out for predators. These two critters combine their talents to face the dangers of the reef together.

...and I'll be your eyes
The goby serves as the pistol shrimp's scout. If danger approaches, the goby flicks the shrimp to tell it to get back in the hideout.

You be my arms...

The pistol shrimp's claws allow it to do things that the goby can't. The shrimp digs a burrow for the two of them to share, where they can hide whenever necessary.

Digging through rocks with fins would be a tough task.

Teamwork

The shrimp and the goby spend every day foraging for food side by side, and every night they sleep together in their shared home. Their strengths as a team make up for their weaknesses as individuals.

123

Glossary

Amphibian

A type of animal that can live both in and out of water. Frogs and toads are examples of amphibians.

Antennae

The feelers an insect uses to sense its surroundings.

Bacteria

Tiny living organisms. Some bacteria can cause disease and illness.

Camouflage

The ability of an animal or plant to blend into its environment to avoid being spotted.

Clone

An identical copy of a living thing.

Commensalism

A form of symbiosis that benefits one species without affecting the other.

DNA

The code inside a living thing that tells it how to look, grow, and behave.

Epiphyte

A plant that grows on other plants.

Evolution

How species change over time to better suit the environment they live in.

Fertilizer

Stuff that can be added to soil to make it better for growing plants.

Food chain

A simple way of describing the connections between different species that eat one another. For example, lions eat antelopes, while antelopes eat grass. Nothing preys upon a lion, so it is said to be "top of the food chain."

Fungus

Neither a plant or an animal, fungus includes a variety of living things, from the mold on your old bread to mushrooms.

Gills

The organs fish use to breathe.

Habitat

The place where something lives.

Kleptoparasite

An animal who survives by stealing from others.

Larva

A baby insect.

Mammal

An animal that typically gives birth to live young, produces milk, and has hair or fur. Humans, whales, cows, and bats are all examples of mammals.

Metamorphosis
The process by which some animals transform into their adult forms—for example, a caterpillar turning into a butterfly, or a tadpole turning into a frog.

Mutualism
A form of symbiosis that benefits both species involved.

Nectar
The sweet, sugary liquid produced by plants that encourages animals to visit and pollinate them.

Nutrients
Stuff that's necessary for living things to grow.

Organism
A living thing.

Parasite
A living thing that survives on or in the body of another living thing, growing at the expense of its host.

Parasitism
A form of symbiosis that benefits one species but harms another (the host).

Pollen
The powdery substance a flower produces that gets transported to other flowers during pollination—by animals, wind, and water.

Pollination
How many plants make seeds together, often with the help of animals such as insects.

Predator
An animal that eats other animals (its prey).

Prey
An animal that is eaten by other animals (its predators).

Symbiosis
When different species form a close, long-term relationship—sometimes benefiting all species involved, sometimes not. This book is all about symbiosis!

Venom
A poisonous substance produced by some animals; for example, some species of snake.

Index

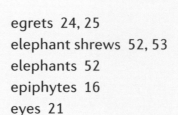

A

acacia trees 94, 95
acorns 100, 101
Africa 22, 26, 40, 52,
    65, 73
algae 42, 43, 104, 105
Amazon rainforest 110,
    111
anemones 32, 33, 114,
    115
anthers 39
ants 6, 18, 48, 84, 94, 110
aphids 18, 19
Atlantic Ocean 34
Australia 116, 117

B

bacteria 54, 55
badgers 8, 9
bald eagles 82
barnacles 46, 47
bats 10, 60, 76
baya weaver birds 82
bee hummingbirds 68, 82
bees 38, 40, 90
beetles 28, 29, 102, 103
Beltian bodies 95
birds 82, 83
blood 14, 26, 56, 76,
    77, 78
blue gum trees 116, 117
booby birds 14, 15
boxer crabs 114, 115
branchiobdellida 50, 51
butterflies 84, 85
butterflyfish 33

C

cacti 96, 97
camouflage 42, 43, 104
cannibalism 85
capybaras 44, 45
carnivorous plants 60
carrier crabs 62, 63
carrion beetles 28, 29
caterpillars 84, 85, 91, 94
cattle tyrant birds 44, 45
chimpanzees 22, 23
chromides 106, 107
clownfish 32, 33
commensalism 86
common tailorbirds 83
corn 98, 99
cowbirds 112, 113
cows 18, 24, 25
coyotes 8, 9
crab spiders 90, 91
crabs 36, 62, 114
crayfish 50, 51
crickets 102
cuckoos 66, 67

D

deserts 96, 97
"devil's gardens" 110, 111
dogs 92, 93
drongo birds 120, 121

E

eagles 82
echolocation 10
eels 70, 71
eggs 6, 21, 66, 74, 96,
    106, 112

egrets 24, 25
elephant shrews 52, 53
elephants 52
epiphytes 16
eyes 21

F

farming 98, 99
fertilization 39
fertilizer 11, 23
figs 10, 11, 22, 23
finches 14, 15
fire 41
flies 28, 29, 45
flowers 38, 68, 90
frogs 6, 7, 102
fruit trees 22, 23
fungus 48, 49

G

Galápagos Islands 14
garbage 37, 87
giant tube worms 54, 55
gills 51
giraffes 17
goby fish 122, 123
gopher tortoises 102, 103
grass 18, 65
great fruit-eating bats 11
great white sharks 118,
    119
green chromides 106, 107
ground squirrels 8, 9
grouper fish 58, 59

H

head lice 56, 57
herbicides 111
hermit crabs 36, 37
hippopotamuses 12, 13
honeydew 18, 19
honeyguides 40, 41
horseflies 45
humans 40, 56, 92, 98
hummingbirds 68, 69
humpback whales 46, 47
hyenas 88, 89

J

jungles 6, 7

K

kleptoparasites 34

L

large blue butterflies 84,
    85
leaf-cutter ants 48, 49
leafflower moths 74, 75
leafflower trees 74, 75
leaf-nosed bats 11
leaves 48, 49
leguminous mulungu
    trees 30, 31
lemon ants 110, 111
lemurs 108, 109
lice 56, 57

lily plants 52, 53
litter 37, 87
lizards 30, 31

M

"mafia birds" 112
manta rays 80, 81
meerkats 120, 121
metamorphosis 74
mites 28, 29
mongooses 72, 73
moray eels 70, 71
mosquitoes 78, 79
moths 74, 75, 105

N

nectar 95, 109
nests 66, 82, 112
nits 56, 57
North America 9, 86
nutrients 55

O

oak trees 100, 101
octopuses 42, 43, 58, 59
orange chromides 106, 107
orchids 16, 17, 78, 79
ostriches 20, 21
ovenbirds 83
owls 102
oxpecker birds 26, 27
oxygen 33

P

pack rats 86, 87
pagoda lilies 52, 53
palm trees 108, 109
parrots 116, 117
pheromones 95
pigs 76, 77
pilot fish 118, 119
pistils 39
pistol shrimps 122, 123
pitcher plants 60, 61
plankton 47
plastic 37
playmates 8
pollination 30, 39, 52, 69, 74, 79, 108, 116
prairie dogs 8, 9
pseudoscorpions 86, 87
puffins 34, 35

Q

queen ants 19, 48

R

rainforest 110, 111
red ants 84, 85
reed warbler birds 66, 67
reefs 70, 122
remora fish 80, 81
rhinos 26, 27

S

sea urchins 62, 63
seabed 42, 43, 54, 55, 58
seeds 10, 11, 22, 23, 109
sharks 118, 119
shells 36, 37
shrews 52, 53
shrimps 71, 122, 123
skinks 30, 31
skua birds 34, 35
skunks 102
sloths 104, 105
snails 36, 37
snakes 7, 102
South America 7
sparrowhawks 67
spider crabs 42, 43
spiders 6, 7, 90, 91, 103
squirrels 8, 9, 100, 101
swift parrots 116, 117
swimming 45
symbiosis 4, 5

T

tails 30
tarantulas 6, 7
Tasmania 116, 117
terrapins 12, 13
ticks 26, 27, 73
tiger orchids 16, 17
tongues 68, 69
tortoises 102, 103
trash 37, 87
traveler's palms 108, 109
trees 82, 83
turtles 12, 13

U

underground habitats 8, 9, 18, 102, 103
urchins 62, 63

V

vampire bats 76, 77
vampire finch birds 14, 15
venom 32, 33, 114, 115

W

warthogs 72, 73
weaver birds 83
whales 46, 47
wildebeests 64, 65
wolf spiders 103
wolves 88, 89
woodpeckers 96, 97
woolly bats 60, 61
worms 50, 51, 54, 55
wrasse fish 70, 71

Y

yellow meadow ants 18, 19
yellow-eared bats 10
yellowthroat birds 112, 113

Z

zebras 20, 21, 64, 65

This has been a

NEON ◆ SQUID

production

Copyright © 2022 St. Martin's Press
120 Broadway, New York, NY 10271

Created for St. Martin's Press by Neon Squid
The Stables, 4 Crinan Street, London, N1 9XW

EU representative: Macmillan Publishers Ireland
Ltd, 1st Floor, The Liffey Trust Centre, 117-126
Sheriff Street Upper, Dublin 1, D01 YC43

10 9 8 7 6 5 4 3 2 1

Library of Congress Cataloging-in-Publication
Data is available.

Printed and bound by Vivar Printing
in Malaysia.

ISBN: 978-1-684-49201-5

Published in February 2022.

www.neonsquidbooks.com

*To my parents, Sheenagh and Brian,
for reading to me.*

Author: Macken Murphy
Illustrator: Dragan Kordić
Consultant: Dr. Ross Piper
US Editor: Allison Singer

A bibliography for this book is available
on the author's website.

Neon Squid would like to thank:

Georgina Coles for proofreading and
Anna Lord for compiling the index.